Historical
AMERICA

The Southeastern States

by
D. J. Herda

The Millbrook Press
Brookfield, Connecticut
The American Scene

Library of Congress Cataloging-in-Publication Data
Herda, D. J., 1948-
Historical America. The southeastern states / by D. J. Herda.
p.   cm.—(The American scene)
Includes bibliographical references and index.
Summary: Examines the history of the southeastern states from
early Indian civilizations through the Civil War to the present day.
ISBN 1-56294-119-4 (lib. bdg.)
1. Southern States—History—Juvenile literature.   [1. Southern
States—History.]   I. Title. II. Series.
F209.3.H47   1993
975—dc20   92-16315   CIP   AC

Cover photos courtesy of: (clockwise from the top):
The Granger Collection; Library of Congress; D. J. Herda.

Photos courtesy of Georgia Department of Industry &
Trade: p. 6; Library of Congress: pp. 8, 16, 22, 27,
35, 39, 47, 49; The Granger Collection: pp. 10, 13,
28, 43; New York Public Library, Astor, Lenox, and
Tilden Foundations: p. 36; D. J. Herda: pp. 53, 54.

Maps by Joe Le Monnier

Published by The Millbrook Press
2 Old New Milford Road
Brookfield, Connecticut 06804

C O N T E N T S

INTRODUCTION

Historical America: The Southeastern States traces the development of the southeastern United States, from the earliest Indian inhabitants through the formative statehood years and on into the twentieth century. The region made up of Virginia, North Carolina, South Carolina, Georgia, and Florida has played a key role in the founding and economic growth of the United States.

In 1619, when the southeastern colonies were struggling for their very survival, the first shipload of African slaves was brought to Virginia. The farmers quickly learned that slaves provided cheap labor for their fields. Before long, tobacco, cotton, rice, and other crops ideally suited to the warm, humid climate of the Southeast were flourishing. These products were in high demand both throughout the colonies and in Europe.

But slavery could not go on indefinitely. By the early 1700s, voices calling for an end to slavery were raised in increasing numbers. In 1808, importing slaves was made illegal by Congress, although farmers still had the right to own and work slaves as they saw fit. By 1840 slavery had been banned in the Northern states, and most Northern slaves had been granted their freedom. But slavery remained an important part of the economy of the southeastern states. Within a few years' time, a growing division had developed between the so-called free states of the North and the slave states of the South.

As new territories were preparing for statehood, pro-slavery forces in the Southeast supported the admission of slave states to the Union. Anti-slavery forces in the North stood flatly against the admission of new slave states. By 1861, this conflict had grown so intense that it led America to war.

When the slaves were freed after the War Between the States, the economy of the southeastern United States did not collapse, as many Southerners had feared. Instead, after a period of adjustment known as Reconstruction, the Southeast began to flourish. The region remains a vital economic and cultural part of the United States today.

THE INDIANS OF THE SOUTHEAST

Long before the coming of the first white explorers, an ancient Indian culture had developed in the fertile farmlands around the central Mississippi River. The culture is called the Mississippian culture after the Native Americans who inhabited the central Mississippi Valley. These Indians included several groups that extended as far east as Georgia, South Carolina, and Florida.

The Mississippian culture was marked by intensive farming, pottery making, temple mound building (similar to the giant pyramids of Egypt), and death cults that involved human torture and sacrifice. The culture reached its peak in the fourteenth and fifteenth centuries, around the time the first Europeans began exploring America. It may have died out as a result of diseases carried by the Europeans to the New World.

All of the Indian tribes of the Southeast were affected by the Mississippian culture. As late as the eighteenth century, various tribes of the region still practiced the Mississippian greencorn ceremony, or busk, offering thanks to the gods for a good harvest. During the ritual, old pottery was smashed, houses cleaned out, and all home fires extinguished. The fires were later relighted from a flame in the main temple.

Many other Mississippian traditions survived among the main tribes of the Gulf region—the Choctaw, Creek, Seminole, and Chickasaw—as well as among the Algonquian and eastern Sioux tribes farther north along the Atlantic coast. Some of these tribes built mounds to serve as house foundations or monuments. They also built temples for worshipping their gods.

(opposite page)
These ceremonial figures used by the Etowah tribe, who lived in what is now Georgia, are representative of the southeastern Mississippian culture.

Like the Mississippian tribes before them, the tribes of the Southeast were mostly farmers. They grew large quantities of maize (Indian corn), sunflowers, pumpkins, melons, and tobacco. For cooking, they occasionally used bear oil or, more often, the oil extracted from the kernels of hickory nuts. They learned how to make hominy and corn breads, as well as persimmon bread, which the first Europeans to visit the area praised highly.

Juan Ponce de León was the Spanish explorer who named Florida. He came to this land in 1513 in search of a legendary "fountain of youth."

Unlike modern-day farmers, the tribes of the Southeast had no domestic animals except dogs, which they were sometimes forced to eat during hard times. Usually, though, there was enough game to supply the meat they required. Through most of the year, the Indians wore little clothing, since the climate was mild. When the nights turned cold, they slipped into soft deerskin cloaks and moccasins and covered themselves with blankets woven from thin strips of bark or the fiber of the nettle plant.

By the time the Spanish explorer Juan Ponce de León came to present-day Florida in 1513, the Indians of the region had already done much of the Spaniards' work. The southeastern tribes had long ago discovered the easiest routes through the mountains and across the rivers. They knew where the best natural shelters lay. They had even located valuable gold and silver deposits and rich mineral springs, which they gladly shared with the newcomers.

They taught early French and Spanish explorers how to build canoes in which to travel the region's many lakes and rivers. They even shared their knowledge of the woodlands with the white man, showing him how to survive in the wilderness and where to find food and drinking water.

The Indians also shared their knowledge of farming with their European brothers. They introduced the Europeans to beans, squash, corn, sweet potatoes, white potatoes, tomatoes, and peppers as well as to such luxuries as peanuts, chocolate, tobacco, and even chewing gum! These were all unknown in Europe before early explorers came upon them in the New World.

The Indians' food crops were much more than mere wild plants harvested from the fields and forests. For hundreds of years, the tribes had slowly been developing improved varieties of plants, much as modern agricultural scientists do today.

The Natchez and their neighbors made high-quality cloth from the fiber of crushed mulberry plants. Nearly all the southeastern tribes were well known for their colorful netted cloaks of turkey feathers. In these respects, the cultures of the southeastern tribes were much more advanced than they appeared to the early Europeans.

FOUNDING THE SOUTHEASTERN COLONIES

By the late 1500s, several wealthy Englishmen were eager to begin founding colonies in North America. They believed there was great wealth waiting to be found in the New World, and they wanted to tap it.

In 1584, Sir Walter Raleigh, a wealthy friend of the queen of England, received permission to gather a group of adventurers to found a colony on Roanoke Island in present-day North Carolina. In April 1585, Raleigh sent one hundred colonists with food and supplies to Roanoke. The leaders of the expedition were given detailed instructions on how to build their colony, but they were not told of the hardships they would face.

Upon landing at Roanoke that August, the colonists set about building shelters. By the time they had completed their task, they realized that they had failed to plant crops to provide them with food for the coming winter. Still, they knew that the local Indians had food, and they were confident that they could trade or purchase whatever supplies they needed. But when winter arrived, they found that the Indians had only enough food for their own survival. Within weeks, the colonists were starving. Fortunately, English explorer Sir Francis Drake stopped at Roanoke Island on a passing voyage. He found the colonists near death and took them back to England in early 1586.

The following year, Raleigh assembled a second group of colonists under the leadership of John White. The colonists arrived at Roanoke Island in 1587. They named their colony Virginia, after Queen Elizabeth, England's unmarried "Virgin Queen."

(opposite page)
When John White returned to the Roanoke colony three years after its founding, all he found was the word CROATOAN carved on a tree. The fate of the Roanoke settlers remains a mystery to this day.

11

White was determined not to make the same mistakes that the first colonists had made. Immediately upon arriving, he gave orders to begin plowing up the land for crops. Within a month, White's daughter, Ellinor, and son-in-law, Ananias Dare, had a baby girl. The baby, named Virginia Dare, was the first English child born in America.[1]

Nine days later, White returned to England. Soon thereafter, England and Spain went to war in Europe, and communications with Roanoke were interrupted for three years. When the war in Europe finally ended, an English ship was sent to check on the well-being of the colony at Roanoke. But when the ship arrived in the summer of 1590, the captain discovered that the colony had vanished. There was no sign of life anywhere. All that remained of the colony were an empty fort, a few trunks, several rotted maps, and a few pieces of rusty armor. A single word was carved on a tree—CROATOAN.

No one aboard the ship understood the word's meaning. Did it refer to the island of Croatoan, which lay to the south of Roanoke? Perhaps the settlers had decided to move there, as they had discussed in the past. Or had the settlers been attacked and killed by the Croatoan Indians? Were they stricken by some fatal disease? And if so, where were their bodies? There were no graves.

The English ship returned to Europe before anyone could solve the puzzle. The question of what happened to the second Roanoke colony remains unanswered to this day.

THE SETTLING OF JAMESTOWN

Despite the tragedy at Roanoke, the English were more determined than ever to found a successful colony in America. But by now they had come to realize that founding a colony was much too costly and risky a venture for one man alone to bear. Raleigh had lost a fortune in trying to start his Roanoke colonies and had nothing to show for his efforts.

In 1606 a group of English merchants decided to form a joint-stock company, similar to a modern-day corporation, to fund their next attempt at colonization. Instead of one person risking all the money required, several people each put up part

of the money and received a share of ownership. Each owner received a certificate, called a stock, or share.

The merchants called their joint-stock company the Virginia Company of London. They received a charter from the king, who told them where they could build their new colony. The Virginia Company then began advertising for strong men to sail to America to help build this new colony. Once in America, the men were to send furs, lumber, and other products back to England for the Virginia Company to sell.

Looking forward to adventure and a chance to share in the wealth of the New World, 120 men and boys signed up to be colonists in the Virginia Company's new venture. (Women were not allowed to accompany them because the trip was by now considered too dangerous.) On a cold, gray day in December 1606, the colonists set sail from London for America aboard

The founding of Jamestown in 1607. After limping along for several years, the colony began to prosper as a center for tobacco production.

13

three ships—the *Susan Constant*, the *Discovery*, and the *God-speed*.

The journey to America proved much more difficult than anyone had imagined. Rough seas and strong winds slowed the ships' pace. Fifteen people died en route. Finally, in April 1607, after more than four months at sea, the ships reached Chesapeake Bay. The settlers chose a place on the banks of a nearby river for their colony. They believed this site would be easy to defend against the savage Indians they had heard so much about from early explorers.

The settlers quickly built a fort, several thatched huts, a storehouse for their food and supplies, and a church. They named the settlement Jamestown in honor of King James I.

But the settlers of Jamestown could not have picked a worse place to build their colony. Instead of choosing an island, as they had been instructed, they selected a peninsula. There, they believed, they could defend the narrow neck of land against attacking Indians, but they soon found they could not defend themselves against an even deadlier enemy—swarms of hungry mosquitoes hatching out of the neighboring swamps. The peninsula turned out to be the perfect breeding place for the disease-carrying insects.

The air surrounding the site proved to be another problem. It had been warm and pleasant enough in April, but it turned hot and humid by summer. And the thick woods that surrounded the settlers had to be cleared by hand—tree by tree—before planting could begin.

As if that weren't bad enough, the settlers were poorly prepared for the hard work that lay ahead of them. Two thirds of them were from the wealthy "gentleman" class in England. They had never worked with their hands in their lives, and they didn't plan to start now. The other third were townsmen who were unfamiliar with farming.

Knowing how important food was to the survival of its colony, the Virginia Company ordered that all provisions be shared equally. Since the colonists believed there would be food enough for everyone whether or not he worked, no one worked very hard. Instead of clearing trees and planting crops, many colonists spent their time searching the riverbanks for gold.

The colonists also turned out to be poor neighbors. Instead of trying to make friends with the Indians, they stole the Indians' corn.

By winter, the food the colonists had brought with them from England was nearly gone. With each passing week, another colonist died from disease or starvation. Of the 105 settlers who had originally landed at Jamestown, only 38 were still alive by Christmas. And the only hope for *their* survival was the promise of more provisions from England.

To the colonists' overwhelming joy, a ship with supplies and new colonists arrived early in 1608, and the colony was spared. Still, it was clear that Jamestown would not survive without a new leader. Luckily for the colonists, that leader was within their own group—Captain John Smith.

JAMESTOWN NAMES A NEW LEADER

Captain John Smith was a man of humble beginnings and rare personal qualities. He had traveled the world as a soldier of fortune and fought bravely in many battles. He had once been sold into slavery in Turkey, but he escaped and eventually made his way back to England.

When the colonists opened their sealed orders from the Virginia Company, they were surprised to learn that Smith had been named as a member of the colony's governing council. Some colonists at first doubted Smith's ability to govern. After all, during the journey to America, Smith had gotten into a quarrel with the company's leaders and been clapped into chains. Shortly after arriving in America, he was captured by the Powhatan Indians and was to be killed. But Pocahontas, the twelve-year-old daughter of the chief, pleaded for his life, and he was spared.

So Smith met with the other council members, but little was accomplished. The council was marred by disagreements and personality clashes from the start. Gradually, though, Smith was able to exert his influence. Before long, he had taken charge of the council. With the colonists on the verge of starvation, he demanded that everyone work for the colony's survival. "He that will not work shall not eat," he announced. He bargained with the Indians for food and other necessities. He

John Smith, an early Jamestown leader, was captured by the Powhatan Indians. Pocahontas, the chief's daughter, is shown here pleading for his life.

convinced the colonists that searching for gold was a waste of time. Yet, despite Smith's best efforts, only fifty-three of the original colonists were still alive by the end of 1608.

The following year, the Virginia Company decided to strengthen the colony at Jamestown by naming a new governor and enticing new colonists from all areas of British society with the promise of free land. The governor, Lord De La Warr (Delaware), sent Sir Thomas Gates to act in his behalf until he could make the journey to America. In May 1609, Gates set sail with a fleet of nine vessels and five hundred passengers and crew. Along the way, Gates was shipwrecked on the island of Bermuda, where he and the other survivors spent the winter in luxury, eating fish, fowl, and wild pigs and basking in the sun until they could be rescued.

Meanwhile, the rest of the fleet sailed on to Jamestown and left off six hundred settlers there. The colony was overwhelmed by the sudden increase in numbers, and mass confusion set in. To make matters worse, John Smith had been injured in a gunpowder explosion and was forced to return to England for treatment. This left the colony without a strong leader, and once again it suffered.

The long, hard winter of 1609–1610 resulted in great food shortages in Jamestown. Supplies that were to come from England failed to arrive. Many colonists, weakened by hunger, fell prey to deadly diseases. By the time Gates and his remaining companions had managed to build two small ships and sail to Jamestown the following May, only about sixty colonists remained. All poultry and livestock, including horses, had been eaten. Some colonists were even said to have resorted to cannibalism to survive! Jamestown was nearly ruined, the Indians had turned hostile, and the decision was finally made to quit the colony and return to England.

In June 1610 the colonists had boarded their ships and were making their way down the James River toward the sea. There they were met by Lord Delaware, who had just arrived with three new ships and 150 men. Delaware convinced the colonists to return with him to Jamestown, and together they built the first new settlements upstream at Henrico (now Richmond) and two more downstream near the mouth of the James.

Jamestown continued to grow slowly until the colony finally discovered what turned out to be its salvation for the future: tobacco. In 1612, John Rolfe had begun experimenting with growing various strains of the crop for export back to England. Finally, he obtained some seed from a passing trader and developed a new strain of mild-tasting tobacco. Before long, tons of the crop were being sent back to England.

That was only the beginning of Rolfe's contribution to the colony's survival. In 1613 a group of colonists under the leadership of newly appointed governor Sir Thomas Dale set out to obtain corn from the Indians. Dale's men captured Pocahontas, hoping to use her as a bargaining point to obtain the corn. Chief Powhatan was furious and threatened all-out war. Rolfe calmly stepped in and proposed marriage to Pocahontas, and a delicate peace resulted. Rolfe's actions may well have saved the colony from extinction.

Finally, in 1619, three events helped spur Jamestown to success. The colony's promoters decided to send wives for the men who, until then, had come to Jamestown to make their fortunes and then promptly return to England. By finding wives for the men, the promoters reasoned, they would add stability to the colony.

The first group of ninety young women who arrived in 1619 were "sold" to likely husbands of their own choice for the cost of their transportation to America, which was the equivalent of about 125 pounds of tobacco.

That same year, the colony had become so prosperous planting and selling tobacco to English markets that it soon began importing labor from the Old World. European whites were brought to America to work as indentured servants on southeastern farms and plantations. These servants were required to work a specific length of time—usually from four to seven years—after which they were granted their freedom.

Later that year, a Dutch man-of-war carrying twenty African blacks who were to be sold as slaves in the West Indies was blown off course. The ship landed at Jamestown and, according to an entry in Rolfe's diary, dropped off "20 Negars," as the black Africans were called. These were the first blacks to reach America. They were sold to the colonists to work as indentured servants. The colonists quickly put the blacks to work in the tobacco fields.

The Dutch traders soon realized that they had found a profitable new market for African slaves. Soon they were bringing regular shipments of blacks to sell to the colonists.

But labor demands in the colonies increased faster than they could be met. Eventually, the colonists realized that they could better meet those demands if they didn't have to free their black servants after just a few years of toil. By purchasing them outright, like cattle or corn, the colonists could own them forever. Since there were no laws banning the ownership of slaves in America, slavery quickly took hold and spread throughout the country.[2]

Another event that helped to insure Jamestown's success was the creation of the House of Burgesses, the colony's first representative lawmaking body. The House met for the first time in a church on July 10, 1619. It was the beginning of self-government in the colonies.

Finally the colony of Jamestown found itself on solid footing. It had a healthy system of representative government, it had plenty of black slaves to work its fields, and it prospered from growing and exporting tobacco to England.

Everything went well for the colony until 1675. Then trouble broke out once again. An argument between a local planter and a group of Doeg Indians on the Potomac River resulted in the Indians killing a plantation worker. In turn, the plantation owner gathered a group of men who tracked down and killed a dozen Doeg and, by mistake, fourteen peaceful Susquehanna Indians.

Before long, a force of Virginia and Maryland soldiers stepped into the fray. In the process, the soldiers killed five Susquehanna chieftains who had come out to talk peace. The remaining Susquehanna braves escaped and soon began attacking frontier settlements along the river. One of the colonists killed by the Indians worked for a man named Nathaniel Bacon.

Bacon was a wealthy colonial planter and the pampered son of a rich nobleman. He quickly gathered a group of neighbors and went out in search of the Indians. They met a group of friendly Occaneechi and convinced them to destroy a small band of Susquehannock. Then Bacon and his group turned on the Occaneechi, slaughtering each and every one.

Hoping to stop the senseless killings once and for all, Governor William Berkeley called for elections for a new town assembly, which met in June 1676. Bacon won election to the council, but he failed to be appointed commander of the army, as he had wanted. In retaliation, Bacon and a small group of men forced Berkeley out of office and set fire to Jamestown. The event came to be known as Bacon's Rebellion. Shortly after, Bacon fell ill and died of swamp fever.

With Bacon gone, Berkeley once again regained control of the colony. He arrested and hanged twenty-three of Bacon's rebels and took control of seven large estates.

When word of the hangings reached London, King Charles II was furious. "That old fool," he said of Berkeley, "has hanged more men in that naked country [America] than I have done for the murder of my own father!" (King Charles's father, King Charles I, had been beheaded in a rebellion in 1649.)

The king recalled Berkeley to England and stripped him of his powers. England then made peace with the surviving Indians, some of whose great-grandchildren still live on small reservations guaranteed to them in a treaty in 1677.[3]

FOUNDING THE CAROLINAS

Meanwhile, in 1629, King Charles I of England had granted a charter allowing Sir Robert Heath to build the first permanent English settlement in present-day North Carolina. The settlement, called Carolina, included all of the land of present-day North and South Carolina. But Heath failed to make use of the land, and in 1663, King Charles II gave a large piece of Carolina to eight of his closest friends.

These people, called proprietors, or landholders, had ambitious plans for making money from their new colony. They were going to give free land to settlers and then tax them heavily. The proprietors' plans called for the settlers to raise olives for oil, grapes for wine, and silkworms for silk. They planned to buy these products from the settlers at a low price and sell them in England for a huge profit.

It would have been a great plan except for one thing: the settlers didn't like it. They refused to go to Carolina if they had to pay a large tax. Neither would they go unless they could have a voice in the running of their own government. Finally, they refused to raise olives, grapes, and silkworms.

In time, the proprietors agreed to give in to the settlers' demands, and in 1670 a group set sail for Carolina, where they built the town of Charles Town (later renamed Charleston).

CHARLESTON PROSPERS

Charleston grew quickly for several reasons. From the beginning, the new colony guaranteed all of its settlers freedom of religion. That proved attractive to English colonists from both Europe and the British West Indies. It was also attractive to Scots, Irish, Germans, and French Protestants, called

Huguenots. The Huguenots were fleeing from France to avoid religious persecution.

Charleston was also blessed by a fine harbor. Before long, trading ships from around the world were stopping at the colony to exchange goods.

Soon other ships began calling on the colony. Pirates, in search of gold and other objects of value, raided the coastal town for the next fifty years. As if that weren't problem enough, hundreds of settlers were killed by Indians during the Tuscarora War from 1711 to 1713.

By the early 1700s, most of the people living in Carolina were split between Albermarle Sound in the north and Charleston in the south. Eventually, the proprietors decided to divide Carolina into two parts, North and South. They gave each colony its own government.

The colony of North Carolina grew very slowly, but South Carolina continued to prosper. Still, the proprietors failed to make a profit from either colony. Meanwhile, the colonists were growing increasingly dissatisfied with the way their colonies were being run. They demanded that King George II take over the colonies. Finally, the king bought back the colonies from seven of the eight proprietors in 1729.

A COLONY OF CONVICTS

By the early 1700s, the English settlements at Virginia, North Carolina, and South Carolina had become well established. Meanwhile, the Spanish had begun settling northern Florida. In order to stop the Spanish advance northward toward the English settlements, the British decided to found still another colony.

In 1732, King George II gave the land between the Savannah and Altamaha rivers to twenty trustees, who named the colony Georgia. This was to be a unique colony. On the one hand, it was to provide convicts and poor English debtors, or people who owed money that they couldn't afford to pay back, a new start in life. It was also to be a haven for religious refugees, who were often persecuted in Europe.

On the other hand, Georgia was to serve as a buffer, or barrier, to the Spanish movement north from Florida. The

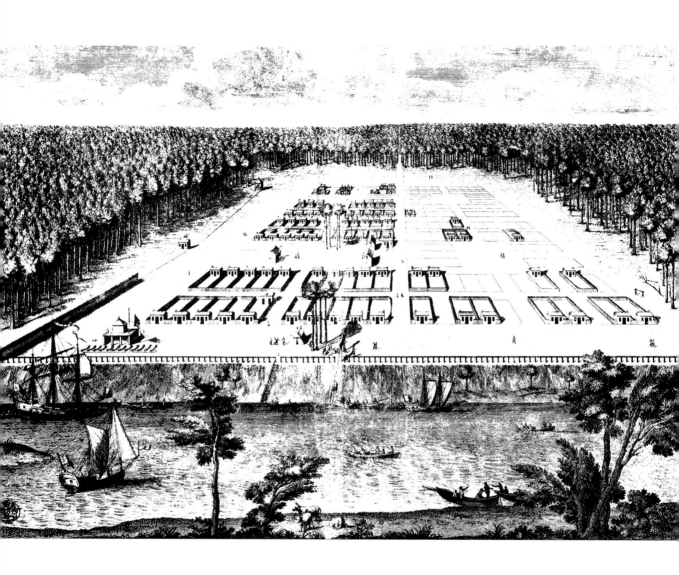

The Savannah settlement was at the heart of the Georgia colony. This engraving shows how houses were clustered in series of blocks, leaving plenty of room for public squares.

Georgia colonists were expected to serve in the military and fight the Spanish whenever necessary. The colony was to be led by General James E. Oglethorpe. Oglethorpe had fought in England for prison reform, so he seemed the perfect man to head a colony of ex-convicts. He was also an experienced military man, so he was well suited to fend off the Spanish.

In 1733 a band of 120 colonists settled near the mouth of the Savannah River. Oglethorpe laid out his new city—called Savannah—carefully, providing for small grids of houses and numerous crisscrossing streets. Many small parks dotted the landscape.

A group of Protestant refugees from Salzburg, Austria, arrived in Savannah in 1734. They were soon followed by a number of Germans and German-speaking Moravians and Swiss. For a time, the colony seemed more German than English. Eventually, groups of Welsh, Scottish Highlanders, Portuguese Jews, and others gave the young colony a worldly character, much like that of its neighboring colony of Charleston to the north.

Savannah succeeded well as a buffer against the Spanish in Florida. But as a means of providing a new start in life for the poor and homeless, it proved a dismal failure. Efforts to develop silk and wine production were unsuccessful. Land holdings were limited to five hundred acres, rum was prohibited, and slavery was forbidden. In addition, strict rules of government turned more people away from the colony than they attracted.

In 1752, a year before the trustees' rights to the colony expired, Georgia was taken over by the king of England and was made a royal province. The regulations against rum and slavery—which were widely disregarded anyway—were dropped, and by 1759 all restrictions on landholding were removed.

By the early 1760s, the colony had begun to grow. Instead of wine and silk, Georgians began exporting rice, lumber, beef, pork, and indigo to Europe. They carried on a rich trade with the West Indies, which lay an easy sail to the south.

At last, the colony that had gotten off to such a late start had become an economic success. And England's thirteen original colonies—the backbone of a country that would later become the United States of America—were thriving.

0   200 Miles

QUEBEC

Lake Superior

Lake Huron

Lake Ontario

Lake Michigan

Lake Erie

Ohio R.

Delaware R.

Hudson R.

APPALACHIAN MOUNTAINS

VIRGINIA

La Fayette

Rochambeau

Washington and

Graves

Chesapeake Bay

ATLANTIC OCEAN

Yorktown
Oct 6-19, 1781

Great Bridge
Dec. 9, 1775

Greene

Guilford Courthouse
Mar 15, 1781

Grasse

Kings Mountian
Oct 7, 1780

NORTH
CAROLINA

Cornwallis

Cowpens
Jan 17, 1781

Camden
Aug 16, 1780

Cornwallis

Moore's Creek Bridge
Feb 27, 1776

SOUTH
CAROLINA

GEORGIA

Charleston
May 12, 1780

Cornwallis and Clinton

Savannah
Dec 29, 1778

Campbell

Major Southeastern Battles of The Revolutionary War

→ Colonial and allied campaign

→ British campaign

✕ Major Battle

The 13 colonies

Other British territories

BREAKING AWAY FROM ENGLAND

All was not going well for the British colonists in America. For years, England had been treating its American colonies unjustly. Britain's Parliament had passed several unpopular taxes on the colonists, forced them to feed and house British soldiers, and refused to hear their grievances. Worse still, the American colonists were English citizens, yet they had no vote for members of Parliament and thus had no say in the running of their own colonial governments. It was only a matter of time before the colonists rebelled.

The rebellion began innocently enough in Massachusetts on April 19, 1775, when two small military skirmishes broke out at Lexington and Concord. In a matter of weeks, the skirmishes had grown into a full-scale war. The colonists, who at first simply wanted more rights as Englishmen, soon realized there was only one route open to them—total independence from Great Britain. Parliament, on the other hand, viewed the fighting as an insurrection, a revolt by a few dissatisfied troublemakers. Even King George III believed the rebels could be put down quickly and law and order restored to the colonies.

Although most of the southeastern colonists firmly supported the Revolution, little fighting took place in the region for the first year that the war raged.

Then, in early 1776, a group of northern Indian tribes, which included the Shawnee, Delaware, and Mohawk, convinced the southern Cherokee to begin striking at frontier settlements in Virginia and the Carolinas. With the outbreak of war between England and America, the Indians saw a perfect opportunity to stop the Americans from expanding onto Indian lands and to regain some of the land they had already lost. With the full support of the British, the Indians began staging raids against American settlements throughout the Southeast.

In August, a force of South Carolina volunteers responded by attacking and burning the lower, or southernmost, Cherokee towns and destroying all the corn they could find. Meanwhile, Virginia and North Carolina forces brought similar attacks against the middle and upper, or northernmost, Cherokee villages. By weakening the major Indian tribes along the western frontier, the Americans hoped to put a stop to the aid the Indians were providing to British forces. In the process, the colonials were also helping to clear the way for rapid settlement of the western region once the war came to an end.

THE WAR IN THE SOUTH

By the end of 1778, the British had shifted their attention from the northern to the southern colonies. England's King George believed that once British troops were on the scene, many Loyalists (American colonists who supported the king and England) would pick up arms in defense of the English crown. In December 1778, 3,500 of Lieutenant Colonel Archibald Campbell's British troops from New York and New Jersey launched an attack on Savannah, Georgia. There they met so few Continental (American) soldiers that they quickly overwhelmed the town. General Augustine Prevost and his Florida Rangers then turned toward Augusta, Georgia, and quickly captured the town. Soon the entire region was under British control.

(opposite page)
The Battle of Kings Mountain, in which the British general Cornwallis was forced to retreat into South Carolina, would later be seen as the turning point of the Revolutionary War.

Then General Henry Clinton, the supreme commander of British forces in America, brought new naval and land forces south to join a massive sea attack that bottled up General Benjamin Lincoln and his large army of American Patriots (colonists rebelling against English rule) on the Charleston peninsula. On May 12, 1780, Lincoln was forced to surrender the city of Charleston. More than five thousand Continental Army soldiers turned themselves in to British forces. It was the largest single American loss of the war.

Congress was stunned by the crushing defeats. Could no one stop the British in the Southeast? Against General George Washington's wishes, Congress decided to place Horatio Gates in control of all American forces in the region. Washington, a native Virginian, was commander in chief of the Continental Army, and he had done a remarkable job of mustering his ragtag troops of farmers and shopkeepers against the mighty British Empire. But Congress felt it was time for a change. Gates, who had been a popular war hero during the Saratoga, New York, campaign of 1777, seemed to be just the right man.

But the British under General Charles Cornwallis surprised Gates's forces at Camden, South Carolina, and sent the American army scurrying north. The retreat was led by Gates himself all the way back to Hillsborough, North Carolina, some 160 miles away. It was yet another staggering defeat for the young Continental Army.

With Georgia and South Carolina nearly completely under British control, the British set out to capture the last Patriot

On January 17, 1781, Patriot troops overwhelmed onrushing redcoats at the Battle of Cowpens.

stronghold in the region—the rugged mountainous area just south of Charlotte, North Carolina. But the "overmountain men" learned of British cavalry leader Patrick Ferguson's plans and, joining forces with other backwoodsmen, caught up with Ferguson and his troops at Kings Mountain. There, on October 7, 1780, they destroyed a British force of 1,100 men.

Overjoyed with a major victory at last, the young Patriots soon received more good news. Congress had named a new commander for the war in the South—General Nathanael Greene of Rhode Island. A seasoned warrior of great patience, Greene was well skilled at managing men and saving supplies, which were growing desperately short in the South. From Charlotte, where he arrived in December, Greene moved his army east toward the Pee Dee River to a site picked by his engineer, Polish volunteer Thaddeus Kosciusko. He then sent a diversionary force of more than 1,600 men under Colonel Daniel Morgan on a sweep to the west of Cornwallis's headquarters at Winnsboro. As Morgan took a position near Cowpens to await the British, he was surprised by the arrival of hundreds of American militiamen anxious to join the coming battle.

Finally their wait paid off. The British arrived, led by seasoned cavalry officer Banastre Tarleton. The two armies faced one another across an empty field and opened fire. After more than an hour, Morgan called for his troops to make an adjustment at their line, and Tarleton mistook the troops' movement for a retreat. He ordered his men to rush the Patriots, who caught the British in a cross fire. Musket balls and powder filled the country air. Tarleton and a handful of cavalrymen managed to escape, but not until more than a hundred British soldiers were killed and six hundred taken prisoner.

From there, Morgan withdrew his troops to North Carolina, where they joined General Greene's main force before returning south to reengage Cornwallis's army. At the Battle of Guilford Courthouse on March 15, 1781, Greene placed his militiamen at the front of the battle line. He ordered them to fire only three shots each at the advancing British and then retreat.

Greene's plan worked perfectly. When Cornwallis's troops saw the Americans withdrawing and took pursuit, Greene's army caught them in a heavy cross fire. After a quick, bloody battle, the American general ordered his troops to retreat. When the fighting was over, Cornwallis was left in possession of the field, but at a cost of nearly one hundred dead soldiers and more than four hundred wounded.

When word of Cornwallis's "victory" reached London, parliamentary leader Charles James Fox was furious. "Another such victory," he told the members of Parliament, "and we are undone."[1]

By using similar hit-and-run tactics, General Greene soon

succeeded in reducing British control in the Southeast to two
strongholds—the cities of Savannah and Charleston.

CORNWALLIS IS NAMED COMMANDER

Concerned about the American successes in the war, the king
of England named General Charles Cornwallis as commander
of all British troops in America in 1781. Cornwallis's forces
joined with those of British general Benedict Arnold, who had
escaped from service in Washington's Continental Army and
defected to the British. The combined number of the two British forces rose to 7,200, far more than the small number of
American troops nearby.

When American reinforcements arrived under the leadership of Anthony "Mad Dog" Wayne, Cornwallis decided to
move his troops back toward the coast, where they would be
safe. From there he planned to march north from Virginia to
join a large British force in New York. Cornwallis set up his
base camp at Yorktown, Virginia, located on a small strip of
land surrounded by the Chesapeake Bay. There he felt secure.
British troops guarded the only land route to the camp, and the
British Royal Navy patrolled the American coastline. America
had no real navy of its own—only a small group of fishing
boats Washington had armed during the siege of Boston. No
number of fishing boats in the world was a match for the
mighty sea power of the British.

At Yorktown, Cornwallis developed a plan. He would call for
the British navy to bring him fresh troops and supplies. With
new troops, he would be able to set out and destroy what
remained of Washington's tired and demoralized army. From
Yorktown, he would send half of his troops north and the rest
south. Once Washington's army was split in two, it would be
little work to defeat the American forces.

Meanwhile, Washington was busy making plans of his
own. In 1778 he had persuaded the French to join the war on
the side of America. Now he asked them to join the American
forces in New York. From there, they would swing south to
Yorktown to form a ring around Cornwallis's troops. Meanwhile, a fleet of twenty-eight French warships would sail into

Chesapeake Bay to keep the British supply ships from coming to Cornwallis's aid.

THE BEGINNING OF THE END

As the plan swung into action, Washington found himself with 17,000 men—more than twice the number in Cornwallis's camp. For the first time in the war, the Americans outnumbered their enemy.

Slowly the combined French and American troops moved closer to Yorktown. Each day the ring they had drawn around Cornwallis grew tighter. Cannons roared around the clock. Musket fire split the cool night air. Meanwhile, the French ships had succeeded in blockading the harbor, just as Washington had planned. Cornwallis was trapped. It was useless for him to fight any longer. On October 17, 1781, the British general surrendered.

The Battle of Yorktown was the last major battle of the war. Peace talks began one year later, and on September 3, 1783, the Treaty of Paris was signed between Great Britain and the United States. Under the treaty, Great Britain agreed that its former colonies were now "free and independent states." Great Britain surrendered all of its American land as far west as the Mississippi River. The American Revolution was over. While the South had been slow to join the war, it had proved critical to America's success.

Historians soon began calling the Battle of Kings Mountain the turning point of the war. Certainly it was the turning point of the southeastern campaign. Even more important, it was a key event in the movement toward American independence.

The war had raged in America for more than six long years. But its conclusion did not mean the end of all problems for the young nation. The original thirteen English colonies—including the southeastern colonies of Georgia, North and South Carolina, and Virginia—were now thirteen United States. In time, a group of delegates would meet in Philadelphia, Pennsylvania, to revise the Articles of Confederation—the constitution that governed the country from 1781 to 1789. Instead, they would make a bold decision to cast aside

the Articles and set about writing an entirely new constitution
—one that provided for a stronger central government.

In the greatly expanded document, each state would be allowed to maintain its own separate government. Yet each would become part of a larger federal government that had the power to enact laws for the good of all U.S. citizens.

While this division of federal and state governments would work well at first, in time it would lead to serious problems. The southeastern states would eventually grow distant from those in the North. While the industrial states of the North moved quickly to ban slavery, the southeastern states grew more and more dependent upon the free labor that slavery provided for its agricultural economy.

At first, this split between free and slave states appeared to be little more than a difference in philosophies. But in time, it would grow to become a major factor in the steadily widening rift between North and South. In time, it would lead to civil war.

CHAPTER FOUR

BUILDING THE SLAVE SOUTH

The slave trade in the Americas got its start long before the first black Africans were brought to Jamestown in 1619. As early as the fifteenth century, Portugal had established Europe's first ties with West Africa for the purpose of trade. The Portuguese came to Africa looking for ivory and gold. By the early sixteenth century, the Portuguese were shipping 170,000 gold coins a year from West Africa to Portugal. In exchange, they traded cloth, wheat, and metal utensils to the Africans.

But gold was not all that the Portuguese took back with them from West Africa. As early as 1444, the Portuguese had begun importing African slaves, who were brought to Portugal to work as household servants.

During the sixteenth and early seventeenth centuries, the demand for cheap labor in Europe's new colonies increased greatly. Laborers were needed to work the metal mines of South and Central America, as well as the sugar and tobacco plantations in the West Indies and South America, where several European countries had colonies. Many colonists— especially in the South—chose to solve this labor shortage problem by importing black slaves from Africa. Soon, Portugal, Spain, Holland, and England were shipping large numbers of African slaves to European colonies around the world. The international slave trade had begun.

White Europeans weren't the only people enslaving black Africans. Many West African kings and wealthy merchants also joined in the growing slave trade. They captured, enslaved, and delivered large numbers of Africans into slavery for a handsome profit. Still, the Europeans were the true power behind slavery. They often armed the soldiers of West African princes and merchants to allow them to capture entire tribes of black Africans—as many as tens of thousands a year. The captives were placed in chains and forced to march to the "Slave Coast" near Benin on the Gulf of Guinea. Many died along the way. Those who survived were placed in large slave pens. Jean Barbot, a seventeenth-century French trader in West Africa, described these pens:

"As the slaves come down to Ouidah from the inland country, they are put into a booth or prison built for that purpose near the beach, all of them together; and when the Europeans are to receive them, they are brought out into a large plain, where the ships' surgeons examine every part of every one of them, to the smallest member, men and women being all stark naked. Such as are allowed [judged] good and sound are set on one side . . . ; [each] is marked on the breast with a red-hot iron, imprinting the mark of the French, English, or Dutch companies so that each nation may distinguish their own property, and so as to prevent their being changed by the sellers for others that are [in worse physical condition]. . . . In this particular, care is taken that the women, as the tenderest, are not burnt too hard."[1]

Once they had been purchased and branded by their new European owners, Africans were packed below deck in wooden sailing ships. As many as one out of six would die from malnutrition, disease, or suicide.

Ships that traveled the slave route between Europe, Africa, and America were nearly always filled with cargo. They carried cheap European goods such as cotton, alcohol, metal, and firearms to the West African coast. There, the slavers traded the goods for Africans, who were transported on the same ships to the West Indies or America and exchanged for sugar and tobacco. These products, produced increasingly by slave labor, were then carried back to Europe to satisfy a rapidly expanding market there. This "triangular trade" between Europe, Africa, and the Americas helped to assure huge profits for everyone involved and kept the slave trade going.

This illustration depicts the first slaves to arrive in chains on the docks of the Virginia Company's settlement at Jamestown.

THE PLANTATION SYSTEM

The large number of slaves in the Southeast soon led to the establishment of huge farms dedicated to growing a single

A TOBACCO PLANTATION

It was on the tobacco plantations of the Jamestown colony that growers first used enslaved Africans as a source of free labor.

crop—usually tobacco or cotton. These farms were called plantations.

Life on a plantation was quite different from life anywhere else in America. Each plantation was more like a small village or town than a modern-day farm. Its main building was the Great House. This was where the planter and his family lived.

It was often built near a river down which the owner shipped his tobacco or other goods to market.

Behind the Great House, near the kitchen, were the vegetable gardens and orchards. Off to one side was the carriage house. Farther away were the work buildings, which included the barns, tool shed, horse stables, and various buildings in which the tobacco was dried, or "cured." Off some distance from the Great House were the slave quarters, where the plantation's slaves lived, usually in one-room cabins. Other buildings included the overseer's house and various shops for candlemaking, soapmaking, blacksmithing, and spinning and weaving.

Since plantations were often very large, southeastern planters often lived quite far from one another. When guests came from a neighboring plantation, they frequently stayed for several days. During their visits, they would be entertained with dancing, fox hunting, card games, and horse races, a favorite pastime of Southern planters.

By the early 1700s, most Southern slaves worked in the fields, but some did other work. On a large plantation, a small number of slaves became skilled carpenters, blacksmiths, brickmakers, and barrel makers. Others lived and worked in the Great House with the master's family. These were the servants who cooked, cleaned, watched after the master's children, and did other household chores.

THE GROWTH OF SLAVERY

By the mid-1770s, slavery had become well established throughout most of the southeastern states. There were several reasons for its rapid growth. Slaves were slaves for life. All of the children of slaves were also slaves. Once a slave owner purchased a black male and several females, his labor problems were over. Within a matter of years, he would have a constant supply of free labor to work his fields, run his household, and do whatever other work was required.

Most southeastern whites considered slaves to be nothing more than property. It was common to hear a slave owner talking about his possessions, which might include "thirty horses, ten mules, six wagons, twelve buildings, and twenty-three slaves." Like any property, slaves could be bought, sold, or traded to other slave owners.

Slaves were also denied all legal rights. While the rights of their masters were protected by the U.S. Constitution and various state and local laws, slaves were forbidden to own any property (including money) or to leave their plantation without a pass signed by their master.

In this way, whites were able to maintain strict control over their slaves. If a slave somehow managed to escape, the power to capture and return him to his owner was guaranteed by law. Many slaves who tried to escape were treated severely upon their capture. They were often whipped and sometimes mutilated by branding. In fact, a slave owner could go so far as to kill a troublesome slave (although few did, because it would mean a loss of valuable property)—all without fear of prosecution.[2]

Slaves were also forbidden by law to marry. Instead, they were forced to breed like cattle or any other form of livestock. And, like livestock, slave families were rarely taken into consideration when an owner needed to raise cash by selling some of his slaves at auction.

Not even Georgia, whose original charter did not provide for slavery, could resist the lure of wealth that slavery had brought to the rest of the Southeast. As more and more farmers began to grow rice, the colony found that it needed more laborers to tend the fields. After Georgia became a royal province in 1752, the ban on slavery was removed, and a plantation economy like that throughout the rest of the Southeast quickly developed.

Despite Georgia's late start in slavery, many slave owners there soon began treating their slaves as brutally as elsewhere in the region. Hard work, poor diets, and severe mistreatment resulted in a high death rate among Georgia slaves. Throughout the Southeast, it was brute force that maintained the slavery system.

While rice plantations grew throughout Georgia, another slave system was developing in the bustling colony of Charleston, the largest port city in the Southeast. By the 1720s, many of Georgia's most successful rice planters had turned the operation of their plantations over to the care of overseers and moved to Charleston. There they bought great mansions on

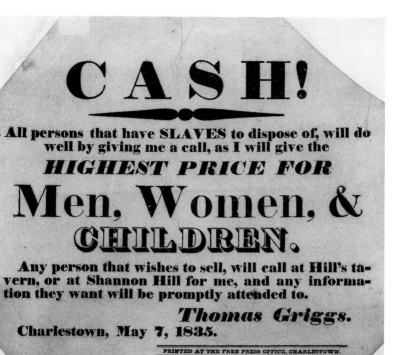

CASH!

All persons that have SLAVES to dispose of, will do well by giving me a call, as I will give the

HIGHEST PRICE FOR

Men, Women, &

CHILDREN.

Any person that wishes to sell, will call at Hill's tavern, or at Shannon Hill for me, and any information they want will be promptly attended to.

Thomas Griggs.

Charlestown, May 7, 1835.

PRINTED AT THE FREE PRESS OFFICE, CHARLESTOWN.

the river, where they could enjoy the milder climate and more "civilized" society. Soon, an aristocracy, or upper-class society, developed. And the luxurious life-style of these aristocrats depended upon slave labor.

Unlike plantation slaves, many city slaves were highly skilled and well educated. Some were of mixed English and African descent. By 1775, half of Charleston's 12,000 residents were blacks. Not surprisingly, they enjoyed greater freedom of movement than plantation slaves. Some of these urban slaves in time were given the opportunity to buy their freedom. Most, however, remained the property of their masters. If they made the mistake of straying too far from the traditional roles of slaves, they would quickly find themselves bound in cuffs and headed back to the plantation in Georgia.

By the early 1800s, anti-slavery sentiments throughout the United States—and even among some people in the slave Southeast—were growing stronger. Northern states had long

A slave trader advertises his services as a buyer of human beings.

ago banned the practice of importing slaves and eventually freed their enslaved blacks. But to the southeastern colonies, slavery was still the base upon which their economic fortunes were built. To the wealthy plantation owners of Virginia, Georgia, and the Carolinas, the protests from the North over slavery were hardly welcome. Southern politicians in Congress, backed by the wealthy plantation owners who supported them, defended the right of planters to own slaves.

But times were changing. Although few slave owners in the Southeast realized it, slavery was destined to come to an end.

A REGION IN TURMOIL

By the early 1800s, the Seminole Indians had been living in peace in Spanish Florida for years. They worked large farms, and some even owned black slaves—just as white slave owners to the north did, although the Indians treated their slaves much better than the whites did.

Eventually, slaves in Georgia learned by word of mouth that Florida slaves were living better lives under their Seminole masters. Inspired by this news, the slaves of Georgia began fleeing their plantations in search of freedom in Florida. Eventually, Georgia slave owners realized what was happening and asked the U.S. Army to step in and help them recapture the runaways.

THE SEMINOLE WARS

In the summer of 1816, a group of U.S. soldiers, backed by the navy, attacked a stronghold of three hundred runaway black slaves on the Apalachicola River in western Florida—a small part of Florida claimed by the United States as part of the Louisiana Purchase. A cannonball from a navy gunboat touched off the slaves' supply of gunpowder. Only fifty blacks survived the explosion. They were eventually returned to their Georgia masters.

In response to the attack, several Seminole war parties staged a series of raids into southern Georgia, where the Indians burned plantations, freed black slaves, and stole horses and supplies. The Seminole raids were met with a number of government reprisals into Florida.

Finally, in December 1817, Secretary of War John C. Calhoun ordered Andrew Jackson to lead nearly three thousand soldiers, Georgia volunteers, and Creek Indian scouts to pacify the Georgia-Florida border. After seizing the old Spanish town of St. Marks on April 29, Jackson ordered the execution of two Creek chiefs and two British traders. He had accused all four of aiding the Seminole in their attacks on Georgia.

The execution created an international scandal. Both Spain and Great Britain demanded that Jackson be punished. Instead, President James Monroe and Secretary of State John Quincy Adams used Jackson's raid as a means of obtaining Florida from Spain by demanding that the Spanish either keep the Seminole under control or sell Florida to the United States.

Believing that the United States was getting ready to launch an invasion of Florida, Spain decided to sell. In addition to acquiring Florida for $5 million, the United States received all Spanish-held land north of present-day Mexico and west to the Pacific Ocean.[1]

The United States suddenly found itself stretching from the territory of Maine in the north to Florida at the very southernmost tip of the continent (although the Seminole had such a strong hold on southern Florida that it would be years before settlers could safely move there). More important, the Georgia-Florida border had been secured by U.S. troops, and the plantation owners there could return to the business of raising crops without having to worry about runaways and Indian raids.

NORTH AGAINST SOUTH

But the outcome of the Seminole Wars only made the abolitionists in the North more determined than ever to end slavery once and for all. They began pressuring Congress to admit new states to the Union as free states—states in which slavery was banned.

A series of political compromises after 1820 succeeded in easing the turmoil of slave versus free labor, but it did not resolve the problem of the growing conflict between pro- and anti-slavery forces. The social values and economic successes of most Northerners revolved around a system of free labor. Northerners believed in economic and social independence

*(opposite page)
During the lifetime of the Seminole leader Osceola (c. 1804–1838), President James Monroe used wars between the Seminoles of Spanish Florida and Georgia to force Spain to sell its land to America.*

and the right of all Americans to move freely around the country. After all, if Northern factory owners had to pay their laborers for work, why should southern plantation owners be any different? Why should the southeastern states be allowed to grow rich and powerful on the sweat and toil of slaves?

The values of most southeastern planters, on the other hand, were quite different. Planters believed that their economic and social welfare was made possible only by the enslavement of blacks.

In 1820, in an effort to ease the tensions between pro- and anti-slavery forces, Congress reached an agreement that allowed Missouri Territory to enter the Union as a slave state, while all territories north of Missouri's southern border would enter the Union as free states. This agreement, called the Missouri Compromise, defused the question of slavery for several decades.

But the Compromise of 1850, a group of acts passed by Congress, overturned the Missouri Compromise by trying to satisfy both the South and the North. Among other things, this Compromise gave new territories the right to decide whether they would allow slavery or not. Then, in 1854, Congress passed another law called the Kansas-Nebraska Act. This law allowed the citizens of these two new states to vote on whether their state would be free or slave.

Senators from the southeastern states (including Florida, which entered the Union in 1845) were furious. They feared that a majority of anti-slavery forces would settle the new states, thus ensuring that they entered the Union as free states and shifting the balance of power in Congress away from the politically strong Southeast and toward the North. Tensions increased when the Republican Party nominated Abraham Lincoln, an outspoken opponent of slavery, to run for president of the United States. Southerners feared that if Lincoln was elected, he would ban slavery across the nation.

"As I would not be a slave," Lincoln once said, "so I would not be a master." On another occasion, Lincoln commented to a friend, "Whenever I hear anyone arguing [for] slavery, I feel a strong impulse to see it tried on him personally."[2]

Lincoln was elected president in November 1860. One month later, South Carolina seceded, or withdrew, from the

44

PENN.

Philadelphia

ILLINOIS INDIANA OHIO

N.J.

MD.

Washington, D.C.

Bull Run
July 21, 1861
Aug 29-30, 1862

Cincinnati

St. Louis

WEST
VIRGINIA

Wilderness
May 5-6, 1864

Fredericksburg
Dec 18, 1862

Louisville

Spotsylvania
May 8-12, 1864

Cold Harbor
June 3, 1864

Ohio River

MISSOURI

KENTUCKY

Richmond

Chancellorsville
May 1-4, 1863

VIRGINIA

Hampton Roads
Battle of the Ironclads

Missouri River

Appomattox
Court House
Apr 9, 1865

TENNESSEE

NORTH
CAROLINA

Memphis

Chickamauga
Sept 19-20, 1863

SOUTH
CAROLINA

ARKANSAS

Tennessee River

Kennesaw Mt.
June 27, 1864

Columbia

Atlanta

MISSISSIPPI

Mississippi River

ALABAMA

Sherman's March
Through Georgia

Ft. Sumter
Apr 12-14, 1861

Montgomery

Savannah

U
N
I
O
N

B
L
O
C
K
A
D
E

LA.

GEORGIA

New Orleans

Jacksonville

Gulf of
Mexico

FLORIDA

ATLANTIC
OCEAN

MAJOR BATTLES
IN THE SOUTHEASTERN
STATES

Union States

Confederate States

N

Major Battles

Major Cities

0   200 Miles

Union. Soon, two more southeastern states—Georgia and
Florida—plus four south-central states—Mississippi, Ala-
bama, Louisiana, and Texas—voted to join it. Virginia and
North Carolina, both of which had strong economic ties to the
North, continued to debate the issue.

Finally, on February 4, 1861, representatives from the six
states that had already seceded (Texas did so in March) met in
Montgomery, Alabama. There they formed a new nation, the
Confederate States of America, in which slavery was not only
accepted but was actually protected by law. The Confederate
representatives chose Kentucky native Jefferson Davis as their
first president. Davis was a cotton planter and a slave owner
who had fought in several military campaigns and had even
served as a U.S. senator from the state of Mississippi. Before
long, the Confederate states began taking possession of military forts and federal-government property within their states,
claiming that these properties now belonged to them.

Lincoln refused to accept the secession of these states and
announced that he would, if necessary, send federal troops to
put down the Southern uprising. But it was too late. In early
April 1861, Union and Confederate forces met at Fort Sumter
on an island in the harbor of Charleston, South Carolina.
Confederate general Pierre G.T. Beauregard demanded that
Major Robert Anderson, the commander of the fort, surrender.
Anderson refused. As time went by, the fort began running
low on supplies. Anderson sent a message to President Lincoln
that he would have to give up the fort unless food and reinforcements were sent soon.

Lincoln told South Carolina representatives that he was
sending supply ships to Fort Sumter. He said that the ships
would not carry guns or troops. He hoped that the Confederates would allow the supplies through and thus avoid a military conflict.

But as the ships approached Charleston, Confederate president Jefferson Davis and his Cabinet met hurriedly in Montgomery. They decided to prevent the ships from reaching their
destination. On April 11, general Beauregard once again demanded a speedy surrender of Fort Sumter. Major Anderson
once again refused. Again Anderson was told to surrender,
and again he refused. Finally, at 4:30 A.M. on April 12, the first

shots rang out at Fort Johnson on James Island. Soon Fort Sumter was under a cross fire from Sullivan's and Morris islands as well. The bombardment continued for thirty hours.

Finally, Anderson's forces ran out of ammunition, and on April 14 they were forced to surrender. Remarkably, the only casualties were two men killed in an accidental explosion during a final salute to the Union flag. But they would not be the last American casualties.

The guns at Charleston had signaled a new era in American history. Lincoln called upon the states remaining loyal to the

On April 12, 1861, Confederates fired on Union soldiers holed up at Fort Sumter on an island in Charleston's harbor. The Civil War had begun.

Union to provide 75,000 militiamen to defeat the Confederacy, an army "too powerful to be suppressed by the ordinary course of judicial proceedings." Volunteers flocked to their recruiting stations. On April 19, Lincoln announced a blockade of Southern ports. The Civil War had begun.

In the furor that followed, four more states voted to secede from the Union—the southeastern states of Virginia and North Carolina plus the south central states of Arkansas and Tennessee.

But Union loyalties in some Virginia communities ran high. In 1863 the residents of the western part of the state voted to secede from Confederate Virginia and form a new state, and later that year Congress admitted West Virginia to the Union.

Meanwhile, the war—now moving into its third year—was taking a heavy toll on the Southeast. But the worst was yet to come.

In 1864, Union general William Tecumseh Sherman was ordered to move his troops against Atlanta. The Georgia capital had long been a strategic Confederate stronghold and a collection point for recruits, making it one of the most important cities in the Confederacy. On September 1, following two months of bitter fighting, Sherman captured the city. As part of his plan to break the back of the Confederacy, he ordered the city burned.

From Atlanta, Sherman led his 60,000 handpicked soldiers on his infamous March to the Sea, burning or destroying nearly everything in his path. Three months and three hundred miles later, Sherman arrived in Savannah on the Atlantic coast. He had succeeded in cutting the Confederacy in two.

(opposite page) Confederate forces fled Atlanta after this bloody battle. Two and a half months later, Sherman's Union army left the city in flames and made a devastating sweep through Georgia's countryside.

In January 1865, Sherman was ordered north to join Ulysses S. Grant, commander of all U.S. forces, whose troops were moving slowly south toward Richmond, Virginia, the capital of the Confederacy. After three long months of bitter fighting, Sherman reached Raleigh, North Carolina, and was preparing to capture Richmond and its defending troops, which were led by Confederate general Robert E. Lee.

Lee, seeing that he was hopelessly outnumbered and severely outflanked, surrendered to Grant that April 1865 at the Appomattox Court House in Virginia.

The war was over. The Union had won. But it had been a costly victory. After four long years of bloody fighting, the southeastern states lay in ruin. Most of the region's plantation system had been destroyed. The area's economy was shattered. By the time the war finally came to an end, much of the South—not only the southeastern states, but also the newer slave states of Kentucky, Tennessee, Alabama, Mississippi, Louisiana, Arkansas, Missouri, and Texas—had been devastated.

Following the Civil War, each of the defeated Confederate states was required by the federal government to write a new state constitution that was acceptable to the government before being allowed to reenter the Union. Each new constitution had to prohibit slavery. Finally, blacks, who had once made up the very backbone of the plantation system in the Southeast, would be free forever. But their progress would not come easily.

Throughout the next century and a half, blacks in North and South Carolina, Georgia, Florida, and throughout the Southeast would have to fight for their social and economic rights. They would be forced to regain them again and again from a widespread group of racial bigots who were determined to prevent them from enjoying the most precious right of all—the right to be free.

CHAPTER SIX

THE EMERGING SOUTHEAST

The Civil War had been devastating for the southeastern United States. About 250,000 Confederate soldiers lost their lives in the war—nearly three quarters of those from the Southeast. All in all, nearly two percent of the entire U.S. population died on both sides.

Blacks after the war remained poor. While some escaped to the factories and general prosperity of the North, many stayed in the Southeast, working long, hard hours on the same plantations on which they had earlier been imprisoned. But following their emancipation, blacks worked as paid employees or sharecroppers, receiving a share of the harvest in exchange for their labor. They no longer worked as slaves.

Although a few plantations continued to thrive, the old plantation system that had begun with the importing of the first slaves nearly three centuries earlier was dead. Many of the planters' great Southern mansions had been burned during the war. Without slave labor—wage-*free* labor—rebuilding proved impossible.

THE ROLE OF RECONSTRUCTION

Shortly after the end of the war, a period known as Reconstruction saw major changes throughout the South. The states that had seceded from the Union were placed under military rule until their new constitutions could be approved by Congress. Meanwhile, Congress demanded that the rights of blacks be protected in each of the rewritten Confederate states' constitutions. Black males had to be allowed the right to vote (women had not yet received this right) as well as to hold public office.

After a state adopted its new constitution and elected a new government, it had to ratify, or accept, the Fourteenth Amendment to the U.S. Constitution. This amendment guaranteed that all citizens—black as well as white—would receive "equal protection of the law." Once a state had met those requirements, it was allowed back into the Union and all federal troops were removed. By 1870 all of the Southern states had rejoined the Union.

Reconstruction worked well—*too* well in some southeastern states. Unscrupulous adventurers from the North and West (called carpetbaggers) gained control of the black vote and excluded local whites from the administration of state governments in South Carolina, Georgia, and Florida. Blacks who a few years earlier had been slaves now filled some state legislatures. An era of irresponsible state spending—outright theft and plunder in some cases—began. Once again, federal troops were sent to South Carolina, Florida, and several other former Confederate states to remove the carpetbaggers from power and restore the state governments to their rightfully elected officials.

By 1877 the last government troops had been withdrawn from the Southeast, and the Reconstruction period had come to an end. During the next twenty years, many of the rights that blacks had won during Reconstruction were lost. Poll taxes and literacy tests kept many blacks from voting. And blacks were once again being segregated, or separated, from whites in restaurants, hotels, theaters, and other public places by various state and local laws. It would be decades before many of these laws would be struck down by the Supreme Court as unconstitutional and blacks would once again become part of the political process in the South.

THE GROWTH OF THE NEW SOUTH

By the turn of the century, the southeastern United States had undergone several major changes. The early 1900s saw a steady shift of the economies of Virginia and the Carolinas from agriculture to industry. Tourism grew into a major source of income for Georgia and Florida as early as the 1920s. High-tech industries such as space and aeronautics, medicine, and

computer technology blossomed throughout the Southeast during the 1960s and 1970s.

Today, changes in society and economics have resulted in an explosion of prosperity for much of the New South. Southeastern economies continue to shift from agriculture to mining, forestry, and tourism in the rural regions and to manufacturing, research, and industry in the urban Southeast.

Today, the New South boasts some of the fastest-growing cities in the nation. Atlanta, Savannah, Charleston, Jacksonville, Virginia Beach, Tampa, Miami, Charlotte, Richmond, Raleigh, and other southeastern cities have developed strong economic bases similar to those in major cities of the North. In the period from 1980 to 1986, Virginia Beach experienced the

The Southeast has become a mecca for northerners who love to escape to the sunny beaches along its coast.

fastest growth of any of the nation's fifty largest cities. Many other southeastern cities were among the top one hundred.

New military installations and expanding government programs are pumping much needed revenues into the region's state and local economies. With America's continuing movement from the mechanical age into the age of electronics and space, new centers of high technology have boomed in Florida. Shipbuilding is still a major industry in Virginia's Newport News, while Norfolk remains one of America's most important commercial ports.

Meanwhile, North Carolina has grown prosperous from the "academic triangle" that includes the University of North Carolina at Chapel Hill, Duke University, and North Carolina State University at Raleigh, where research and development are devoted to improving America's future. South Carolina has witnessed a similar economic boom with the development of its chemical and paper industries, as well as the large-scale development of its deep-water ports at Charleston, Georgetown, and Port Royal. Georgia, with its moderate year-round climate, enjoys a healthy economic mix of tourism, industry, and agriculture.[1]

Yet, despite its growth, the southeastern United States still shows signs of its unique heritage. Rolling hills, grassy plateaus, sparkling seashores, and towering mountains call out to visitors—just as they did hundreds of years ago. The difference today is that a stroll through the countryside of Virginia or the Carolinas or Florida or Georgia is a walk through the battlefields of history. Men and women fought and died here in the defense of their own way of life. They clashed on land where previous men and women had struggled against the tyranny and oppression of a foreign government to bring the United States into being.

(opposite page)
Although Charleston, South Carolina, has become a major port city, its buildings offer a glimpse of the antebellum (pre-Civil War) South.

STATE FIRSTS

FLORIDA   **Statehood: 1845**

Florida boasts the oldest permanent city in the United States in Saint Augustine. It was founded in 1565 by the Spanish admiral Pedro Menendez de Aviles to stop the French influence at Fort Caroline on the St. Johns River.

The United States purchased Florida from Spain for $5 million in 1819. Andrew Jackson, the military commander of the territory, took part in the transfer ceremony at Pensacola on July 17, 1821.

Commercial sponge fishing was begun at Key West in 1849. Over the course of the next century, Florida led the world in the production of natural sponges.

GEORGIA   **Statehood: 1788**

In 1793, Eli Whitney invented the cotton gin on a plantation near Savannah. It was the first successful machine for separating cotton fiber from its seeds. The cotton gin paved the way for raising cotton on a large commercial scale and opened the era of the sprawling southern plantation.

In 1819 the first transatlantic steamer, the *Savannah*, crossed the Atlantic Ocean from Savannah to Liverpool, England, in twenty-five days.

In 1842, Dr. Crawford W. Long performed an operation at Jefferson using ether as an anesthetic. It was the first time ether had been used in surgery.

NORTH CAROLINA   Statehood: 1789

On April 12, 1776, the Fourth Provincial Congress instructed the North Carolina delegates to the Continental Congress to vote for independence. North Carolina was the first state to do so.

In 1784 the settlers of western North Carolina (present-day Tennessee) set up the temporary state of Franklin when the cession of the territory to the United States left the residents without state or federal protection.

The state's first university was chartered in 1789 and opened in 1795. The University of North Carolina at Chapel Hill is today the oldest state university in America.

SOUTH CAROLINA   Statehood: 1788

Rice was first raised in South Carolina around 1680 when Henry H. Woodward planted some seed given to him by the captain of a passing Madagascar trade ship. Much of the state's wealth was based on the production of rice until the middle of the nineteenth century.

On October 7, 1780, a British force was met and defeated at the Battle of Kings Mountain. The American victory proved to be the turning point of the Revolutionary War in the South.

During the American Revolution, Fort Charlotte was the first British fort to fall to Colonial troops. Nearly a century later, another of South Carolina's installations, Fort Sumter, was the first Union fort to fall to Confederate forces during the Civil War. Fort Sumter was also the site of the first shot fired in the war on April 12, 1861.

VIRGINIA   Statehood: 1788

In 1619, the House of Burgesses, the first lawmaking body in the colonies, assembled at Jamestown. The group's purpose was to help defend the rights of the colonists against the king of England.

On October 19, 1781, General Cornwallis and his British army of nearly eight thousand men surrendered to Washington at Yorktown, bringing an end to the Revolutionary War.

On April 30, 1789, Virginia gave the nation its first president, George Washington. It would take another two hundred years before Virginia would enter the American history books by electing as governor L. Douglas Wilder, the first black ever to hold a state's top office.

Virginia was one of the main battlegrounds of the Civil War. Among the heroic Confederate generals of the state were Robert E. Lee, "Stonewall" Jackson, Joseph E. Johnston, "Jeb" Stuart, J. A. Early, and G. E. Pickett.

N O T E S

CHAPTER TWO
FOUNDING THE SOUTHEASTERN COLONIES

1. Dr. Herbert J. Bass, *Our Country* (Morristown, N.J.: Silver Burdett & Ginn, 1991), p. 154.
2. Ibid, p. 159.
3. George Brown Tindall, *America: A Narrative History* (New York: W. W. Norton & Company, 1984), pp. 146–148.

CHAPTER THREE
BREAKING AWAY FROM ENGLAND

1. Tindall, *America: A Narrative History*, p. 224.

CHAPTER FOUR
BUILDING THE SLAVE SOUTH

1. Herbert G. Gutman, *Who Built America?* (New York: Pantheon Books, 1989), p. 26.
2. Richard T. Schaefer, *Racial and Ethnic Groups* (Glenview, Ill.: Scott, Foresman and Company, 1990), p. 207.

CHAPTER FIVE
A REGION IN TURMOIL

1. Richard H. Dillon, *North American Indian Wars* (New York: Facts on File, Inc., 1983), p. 78.
2. Bass, *Our Country*, p. 429.

CHAPTER SIX
THE EMERGING SOUTHEAST

1. John W. Wright, ed., *The Universal Almanac* (Kansas City, Mo.: Universal Press Syndicate Company, 1990), pp. 164–165.

SELECTED BIBLIOGRAPHY

Bass, Herbert J. *People in Time and Place*. Morristown, N.J.: Silver Burdett & Ginn, 1991.

Casner, Mabel B., and Ralph H. Gabriel. *Story of the American Nation*. New York: Harcourt, Brace & World, 1962.

Gutman, Herbert G. *Who Built America?* New York: Pantheon Books, 1989.

Schaefer, Richard T. *Racial and Ethnic Groups*. Glenview, Ill.: Scott, Foresman and Company, 1990.

Tindall, George Brown. *America: A Narrative History*. New York: W. W. Norton & Company, 1984.

Wissler, Clark. *Indians of the United States*. New York: Anchor Books, 1989.

Wright, John W., ed. *The Universal Almanac*. Kansas City, Mo.: Universal Press Syndicate, 1990.

SUGGESTED READING

Aylesworth, Thomas G., and Virginia L. Aylesworth. *The South*. New York: Chelsea House, 1991.

Beeger, Gilda. *The Southeast States*. New York: Franklin Watts, 1984.

Behrens, June. *A New Flag for a New Country*. Chicago: Childrens Press, 1975.

Bosco, Peter I. *Roanoke: The Story of the Last Colony*. Brookfield, Conn.: The Millbrook Press, 1992.

Dillon, Richard H. *North American Indian Wars*. New York: Facts on File, Inc., 1983.

Freedman, Russell. *Indian Chiefs*. New York: Holiday House, 1987.

Hope, Mary. *Journey South: Discovering the Americans*. New York: Friendship Press, 1980.

Smith, Carter, ed. *A Sourcebook on Colonial America: Battles in a New Land*. Brookfield, Conn.: The Millbrook Press, 1991.

_____. *A Sourcebook on Colonial America: Daily Life*. Brookfield, Conn.: The Millbrook Press, 1991.

_____. *A Sourcebook on Colonial America: The Revolutionary War*. Brookfield, Conn.: The Millbrook Press, 1991.

INDEX